Count...

Attendanc...
Pastora... ...gy

Paddy Benson

Vicar of Barnston and Rural Dean of Wirral North Deanery

John Roberts

Research Associate, Centre for Ministry Studies,
University of Wales, Bangor and
Adviser to the Wirral North Deanery Pastoral Committee

GROVE BOOKS LIMITED
RIDLEY HALL RD   CAMBRIDGE   CB3 9HU

Contents

Acknowledgments

We wish to thank the incumbents and people of the parishes which participated in this survey. We were dependent on their goodwill and hard work. In particular Jonathan Gibbs, Rector of Heswall and incumbent of John's home parish, allowed Heswall to be used to pilot the survey.

We are grateful to members of the Pastoral Committee for their rigorous oversight of the survey's methods and conclusions, and for their encouragement as we prepared this booklet. The Grove Pastoral Series editorial group, especially Gavin Wakefield and Paul Simmonds, have also made important contributions. Responsibility for the commentary and for any errors of fact or inference are, however, ours not theirs.

The Cover Illustration is by Peter Ashton

First Impression December 2002
ISSN 0144-171X
ISBN 1 85174 517 3

Introduction

Who Attends Your Church?

The smaller church attendances these days should have one benefit—you ought to know the names of the people who remain. So how come every week there is someone there you know you should know, but you cannot remember his or her name?

This booklet will suggest that there are many people who attend your church rather infrequently. We have called them 'Casual attenders.' However we believe that it is essential not to be casual in our attitude to them. They are a resource, and a mission opportunity, and also a warning to the church as it plans its pastoral programmes and outreach activities.

Attendance at public worship is not always the best indicator of the church's life and 'reach' into the community. But it is *an* indicator; and in the opinion of many commentators it points to a disastrous decline in the church's size and influence during the course of the last century. Newspaper headlines have sensationalized the fall below one million in Church of England weekly attendance (a figure since adjusted to slightly in excess of one million by a new method of calculating the weekly average).[1] Statisticians have described a catastrophic fall in attendance over the latter part of the 20th Century. *Christian Research* calculates that at present rates, the church could be extinct within a generation.[2] This dramatic fall in weekly attendance has been confirmed both by returns collected by the Archbishops' Council,[3] and by the British Social Attitude (BSA) studies.[4]

Newspaper headlines have sensationalized the fall below one million in weekly attendance

The church has been keeping some form of attendance record for 150 years. A century ago those counted were Easter Day communicants; since then the list has been widened to include Christmas communicants, Sunday attenders (with children now noted separately) and finally, in 2000, mid-week attenders. Latterly there have been attempts to recognize and avoid the distortions of one unusual week, by taking attendance figures for a month and averaging them out to discover average Sunday attendance (aSa). Throughout the whole period, the national and local focus has remained on those who are present on a single Sunday (or, from 2000, a single week), which is all well and good if most regular attenders are present at every count, but misleading if they are not. Of course in reality not everyone can be present every week, but the traditional perception has been that those who are missing are few. Consequently a decline in weekly attendance is interpreted as a definitive measure of a decline in the number of people who meet regularly to worship. However, in 1996 the Board of Mission suggested a different way of reading the church attendance figures:

> There is widespread anecdotal evidence to suggest that 'regular worshipper' now means 'two or three times a month' rather than the former 'once a Sunday'...This change in patterns of church attendance is not reflected in the figures, which may actually be evidence that slightly more people are going to church, but less often.[5]

Data has been collected to supplement this 'anecdotal evidence.'[6] The true situation is more complicated than either the newspaper headlines or the Board of Mission suggest. Congregations have been studied which have some regular worshippers who rarely miss a Sunday, but also other regular worshippers who attend less often, down to once a month. It is quite possible that there are also others who are regular attenders at even lower frequencies—say, once a quarter or once in six months. Many people attend church regularly, but rarely. It helps to explain why you have a problem with names.

A Deanery Attendance Survey

In 2000–2001, the Deanery of Wirral North in the Anglican Diocese of Chester conducted a pastoral review. Every five years each deanery (a group of parishes—in our case, fourteen parishes) audits its work and makes plans or recommendations for the future. This time, the deanery's pastoral committee decided that the audit would take the form of an attendance survey.

The idea for the survey came from John, who was studying patterns of church attendance. He had examined the result of similar surveys which were held in Wakefield, Ripon and Canterbury in recent years. These surveys had produced results which some of our committee (including Paddy) found surprising. Accordingly we asked our parishes to take detailed records of attendances at all their services over an eight-week period.

A deanery is a fellowship, not a command structure. Many of our parishes decided not to take part in the survey. Those that took part used somewhat varied methods of collecting and communicating data. In the end, only seven parishes took part in the survey, and not all of them supplied information under every heading. Nevertheless we believe that what emerged from the survey is of considerable interest, not least because its results raise further questions which deserve proper study.

In Paddy's parish (where six weekly services meet in two churches) the weekly attendance during the eight weeks varied from 265 to 309, averaging 289. However, the number of named individuals who attended during the period was 610. That does not include baptism guests and visitors to the area; add them in, and the total jumps to 880. Paddy's 'worshipping community' is between twice and three times the number he sees on any given Sunday.[7] How do we minister to this moving target? Sermons that begin 'Last Sunday we looked at the background to Romans. I'm sure you remember what was said, so today we'll start straight in at Chapter 2...' miss the point. Last Sunday, half of today's congregation was at work, or out walking the dog.

The Wirral North survey suggested there was a spread of attenders across the entire frequency range from one week in eight, to eight in eight. Ignoring the one-in-eight attenders for a moment, we focus on those who came to church at least twice during the eight weeks (and so could be said to have a 'pattern' of churchgoing).[8] Many of these returning attenders were neither 'once a Sunday' nor 'two or three times a month'...

8/8	7/8	6/8	5/8	4/8	3/8	2/8
11%	15%	13.5%	14%	14.5%	15%	17%

Table 1: Frequency patterns of returning survey
attenders in Wirral North Deanery

...and of course, these are just the 'patterns' that we know about. As suggested above, if we had extended our eight-week survey over twelve weeks or sixteen, we might have found more patterns of repeated church attendance at even lower frequencies. It seems that people attend church when they want to, and not in order to conform to some pre-existing notion of regular church attendance.

How We Conducted the Survey[9]

Parishes were given guidance and, when requested, training in how to conduct the survey. The raw data was in most cases entered on computer in the parish, and then transmitted to John for scrutiny and analysis.[10]

The precise form and manner in which data was collected varied somewhat from parish to parish. However, the following example, from Paddy's parish of Barnston, was typical.

During the survey period at every service (other than weddings and funerals) an A6-size card was handed out for every person who attended. The cards were colour-coded according to the service. Pens and pencils were available in the pews. At some point in the service, the leader announced the purpose of the survey, and asked everyone to complete a card—even those who had completed cards on a previous occasion. (People who had completed a card previously were asked to write in just their name and phone number, to help us identify them unambiguously—they only filled in other details such as address or age if these had changed.) Adults were asked to complete cards on behalf of infants. The cards were collected at the end of the service. Inevitably there were a few who forgot or who chose not to complete cards; but a comparison of the number of cards returned with the overall number of attenders recorded by sidespeople suggests that we had a high completion rate, averaging 96% per week.

Built-In Limitations of the Survey

To collect any information at all, we relied on the honesty, conscientiousness, intelligence and efficiency of several hundred fallible human beings over a two-month period. Only in John's own home parish of Heswall was the process of collecting attendance data put under particularly close scrutiny. However, it is reassuring to find that other parishes' survey profiles were in line with Heswall's results.

Our congregation on any given Sunday will be very different from the whole worshipping community to which we minister

But even if the data was collected flawlessly, there are legitimate questions about how representative and comparable the information is. For example, in any eight-week period some people will be ill, or visiting relatives in Australia, or otherwise departing from their usual attendance pattern. Again, were these 'ordinary Sundays'? None of the parish surveys hit Christmas, but one did run up to Easter. There were parade services (when uniformed organizations attend), baptisms (swelled by large numbers of visiting relatives) half-terms (when the congregation is in Tenerife) and other local factors which affected attendance. This cannot be helped. Every church's life has its own rhythm and there is no such thing as an 'ordinary' Sunday, let alone eight 'ordinary' Sundays in a row. We can only hope that over eight weeks the extraordinary factors more or less average out.

In any case, even after all possible caveats, we believe that our findings are reliable in reflecting this fact: that our congregation on any given Sunday will be very different from the whole worshipping community to which we minister. One effect of the work so far is to whet our appetite to repeat the survey in some of the same parishes. This will tell us whether the same over-all attendance patterns are found a second time. When we compare the names of attenders with those who were recorded the first time round, it may also tell us whether we were broadly correct in our classification of the attend-ance patterns of the individuals in each congregation.

We need to keep the 'snapshot' nature of the survey in mind when we evalu-ate our findings. For example, we describe someone who attended church only once during the survey period as a 'Casual' attender, but applied to an individual case this may be misleading. The person may have come to church because the golf was cancelled; or he/she could be a new missionary who departed overseas after week one. Without more information, we cannot tell anything about the spiritual state of the Casual (or any other) attender.

2 The Survey: Results and Analysis

In what follows, we have not supplied detailed data or all the interesting analyses that can be applied to it because of constraints of space.[11]

We have not included our findings about the gender split of different age-groups and different frequencies of attendance. This information is important, but the results in this area are (to us, anyway) less startling and more space-consuming to set forth than some of the other findings.

Categories and Definitions

The survey data gave us information about the attendance of identified individuals[12] which we chose to analyse by the following categories:

- Gender
- Age-band (under 5, 5–10, 11–16, 17–24, 25–29; 30s, 40s, 50s, 60s, 70+)
- Visitor or not (that is, visitor to the Wirral or ecumenical visitor. From address and respondent's own assessment)
- Baptism guest or not (from respondent's own assessment)
- On parish electoral roll or not (by cross-referring to electoral roll)

We were interested in defining the parish's 'worshipping community.' Merely checking addresses is not enough, as people cross parish boundaries to belong to a church other than that where they live. We used this definition:

- *The worshipping community* comprises those attenders who cannot be identified as baptism guests or visitors to the area (note: the worshipping community is not defined by frequency of attendance or parish of residence).

We asked parishes to indicate which attenders were involved in activities other than merely attending worship—such as teaching in children's groups, reading the lesson, serving on the PCC, joining a housegroup or an *Alpha* Course or being on the coffee rota. We applied this only to adults over 24 years of age. By this somewhat subjective assessment we distinguished between

- *Modal* (church-service-only) participants and *Church Life* participants.

When a person attended any service, Sunday or midweek, they were recorded as attending for that week. No distinction is made here between people who attended one service and those who attended two or more services during the same week—although we have this data on record.

We classified attenders by frequency of attendance:

- *Core:* attended 6, 7 or 8 weeks out of 8
- *Mobile Core:* attended 4 or 5 weeks out of 8
- *Worshipping Fringe:* attended 2 or 3 weeks out of 8
- *Casual attender:* attended 1 week out of 8

A. Overall Church Attendance

Average Sunday Attendance (aSa) and Average Weekly Attendance (aWa)
We began by giving our data the traditional analysis, that is, working out the average attendance for comparison with statistics kept from previous years. Our survey numbers were based on weekly attendance (including midweek worship services) not just Sundays. But on the whole we could extract from our figures a statistic comparable to the previous records.

aWa figures paint a familiar picture to someone accustomed to looking at past years' aSa returns

Our aWa numbers were broadly similar to existing aSa figures. There were a couple of divergences. One parish showed a 30% increase on earlier figures, and another showed a 30% decrease. It is virtually impossible to guarantee that survey periods are strictly comparable from year to year. Our survey was intended to avoid religious festivals and other occasions when large numbers of occasional attenders were likely to attend. However, the previous returns were based on attendance during the first four weeks in October, and are likely to have included Harvest Festival services, which in many cases will have attracted significant numbers of occasional attenders. Despite those blips up and down in two parishes, we are satisfied that the aWa figures derived from the data we collected paint a familiar picture to someone accustomed to looking at past years' aSa returns.

Of course, averages conceal as much as they reveal. At the extreme, a parish with an 'average weekly attendance' of 200 over eight weeks could have 1600 worshippers on week one and nobody at all for the rest of the survey.

We did not record any fluctuations on that scale; but certainly a variation of 12% above and below the average was common. Bebington parish, for example, had an aWa of 358; but their largest weekly attendance was 401, and their smallest was 303. It is sometimes possible to identify local factors linked to these fluctuations. For example, numbers may be swelled by a parade service attended by the cubs (and their parents) or depressed by a large number of people going away at half-term.

Survey Attendance: Different Types of Attender
We then counted the actual, named individuals who make up the average figures in our survey. We found that the number of individuals who attended during the eight weeks of the survey was *more than double* the aWa figure.

Where were all these 'extra' worshippers coming from? Were they, for example, visitors to the church who were not realistically part of the worshipping community? We had asked parishes to identify different types of attender (see 'categories and definitions,' above). Consequently we were able to see that some of the extras were Baptism guests and out-of-area visitors or ecumenical visitors who do not count themselves as part of the congregation.

However, even if a parish had many Baptism guests and out-of-area visitors, they were only part of the reason for the huge disparity between the average weekly attendance figure and the overall number of identified attenders. A case in point is Heswall parish:

- The weekly average was 466 attendances by all attenders
- 1402 individuals were identified
- Only 410 of these were baptism guests
- Only 78 were out-of-area visitors.
- So Heswall had 914 community attenders during the survey, each of whom was identified by name and address. That is more than twice the weekly average of all attenders.

Our survey parishes have different pastoral policies, and come from different social settings. Parishes which operate a firmly disciplined baptism policy had few or no baptism guests; while those with a more open policy had many. Some parishes had many out-of-area visitors; others had few. *But all the parishes surveyed, irrespective of church tradition or policy, had a much larger survey attendance than weekly attendance—typically double.*

B. The Worshipping Community

The Misleading Congregation

In this section we ignore the Baptism guests and other visitors, and focus on the rest of the congregation—the worshipping community. The survey shows us that the congregation in the pews on any given Sunday is not a representative sample of the whole worshipping community. If we judge by appearances, we will be misled.

In any given week, the more frequent attenders will be over-represented in the pews. For example, in Heswall the shape of the weekly community appears as shown in figure 1 below. However, viewed over the full survey period the community takes a very different form, as shown in figure 2.

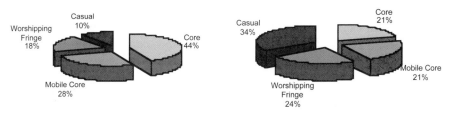

The Congregation Analysed by Frequency of Attendance

Fig 1 Average Weekly Attendance at Heswall   Fig 2 Survey Attendance at Heswall

The weekly congregation is a mixture of people who follow different attendance patterns. For example, 75% of those who attend 6 weeks out of 8 will be present, but only 25% of those who attend 2 weeks out of 8.

A moment's reflection will suggest some areas where this will affect the work of the church. For example

> • Communication—If the weekly service is the only forum for communicating news to the bulk of the community then information given out during a single week is four times less likely to be received by a monthly than a weekly attender.

The least frequent attenders will be outside the circle of church information. They may lack information about practical changes in worship arrangements, forthcoming non-worship activities, or proposed alterations in church matters. They have to take the church as they find it every time they attend, and are excluded from events simply because they do not know what is going on.

- Teaching—Exposition of Scripture and Christian teaching in church or children's groups will be received with different levels of regularity. The coherence of planned or systematic teaching will be lost on many.

Age Divergence Between Weekly and Survey Congregations

The age profile of the population in England has changed considerably in recent years as a result of a reduction in the birth rate and an increase in longevity. However, it has been suggested that age profiles of worshipping communities seem to show even greater change. Some have warned of a serious imbalance between worshipping communities and their local populations. The church, it is said, has no young people.

We compared the ages of individuals in the survey with census data on the age profile of each parish. We found that the worshipping community is indeed older than the local population. However, the age gap between the congregation (viewed over eight weeks) and the local population is much less serious than the common perception, which is based on the weekly community. Since older people are commonly more frequent church attenders, the age profile of the weekly congregation diverges from that of the survey congregation. Fig 3 and Fig 4 below shows the weekly and survey age structures in Frankby parish.

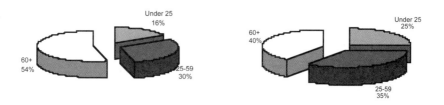

The Congregation Analysed by Age

Fig 3: Weekly Attendance at Frankby   Fig 4: Survey Attendance at Frankby

A misleadingly old-seeming weekly congregation can influence parish policy, for example in the way that services are organized and presented. Decisions may be taken to reflect the perceived wishes or needs of the weekly congregation—but this congregation is disproportionately elderly. The total worshipping community may contain many young adults under forty, but each attends less frequently than their elders. It is easy to identify a range of choices in which a preacher or worship leader may be unconsciously influenced by the predominance of grey heads on any given Sunday morning.

- Choice of music style—traditional rather than modern
- High expectations of Bible knowledge and background derived from Sunday School
- Low expectations of knowledge about current science and technology
- Narrow perceptions of the kind of social pressures and moral dilemmas which the congregation faces

One young age-group was surprisingly well represented, both in the survey congregation and even in the weekly congregation. We found that the percentage of children (from age 5 to mid-teens[13]) in the worshipping community was close to the percentage of children in the local population as a whole. The dramatic fall in the number of children attending children's Sunday groups (from 1,039,000 in 1960 to 88,000 in 2000[14]) has led to concern that our churches are becoming bereft of young people, and there is certainly no reason for complacency. However, the figures suggest that we should not give way to despair, nor overlook our continuing contact with a significant number of children.

The unexpectedly large numbers of children and young people recorded in our survey included a high proportion of Casual attenders. Since children's groups materials and lessons often assume weekly attendance, these Casual attenders are likely to find themselves baffled by what is going on. That is assuming they make it to their group. Casually-attending children may stay with their parents in a main service, and not go out with other children.

Varied Patterns of Attendance
The attenders came to church anywhere from once to eight times during the survey. We were interested to discover that the biggest group (in all but one parish) was the group which attended once only. The groups which attended at other frequencies were usually fairly similar in size to one another. For example, in New Ferry parish the attendance frequencies were as follows:

8/8	7/8	6/8	5/8	4/8	3/8	2/8	1/8	Total
28	33	23	25	26	9	22	63	229
12%	14%	10%	11%	11%	4%	10%	28%	

Table 2: Attendances by the Worshipping Community at New Ferry Parish

These figures show that at New Ferry a relatively large group, 28%, attended once during the survey. Otherwise (apart from the dip at three weeks out of eight) the frequencies are pretty evenly represented. We did not find, for example, that the single-attenders were counterbalanced by a large group of people who came every week. The parishes in our survey differ from one another in tradition and in social composition. But they all show similar attendance patterns in which attenders were distributed across the range.

If non-attendance at church is a problem, then it is a problem which to some extent affects around 90% of the worshipping community of our survey parishes. New Ferry, where 12% had a perfect score of 8/8 attendances, was the top performer in our deanery. The lowest perfect-score figure for church attendance was 4% in one parish. There are many reasons why someone may not attend church, and not all of them are sinister. But if church life is designed around the assumption that all members will be there every week, then we are creating difficulties for most of the congregation.

Where are the Electoral Roll Members?
In theory, we might expect that the most committed, most frequently attending members of a church would also be those on the electoral roll.[15] In our survey, the reality was different. Except in New Ferry (with just 7% of electoral roll absentees), many of those on the electoral roll did not attend church at all during the survey period. Barnston parish was typical: 151 out of 414 electoral roll members (36% of the total) did not come to church during the eight weeks of the survey. Other parishes' electoral roll absentee rates ranged from a quarter to a half of the roll. Electoral roll members who did attend were not necessarily the most frequent attenders. They were somewhat more likely to be frequent attenders than the average, but not overwhelmingly so.

Why should so many electoral roll members attend church rarely or not at all? Electoral rolls remain open for six years, and are then closed and reconstituted according to the requirements of the Church Representation Rules. Once people have joined the roll, they tend to remain members until it is closed and reorganized, irrespective of whether they remain churchgoers. Those who move out of the area should (with their consent) be removed from the roll by the electoral roll officer, as should those who die. However, many rolls accumulate a proportion of other people whose churchgoing practice has reduced or ceased. At the reorganization in 1996 the rolls in four of our survey parishes were reduced by between 20% and 39%. Our survey, taken in 2000–2001, used a four-year-old roll with an accretion of inactive members.

The Church of England suggests that joining an electoral roll should be more than a requirement for administrative purposes. It should be an occasion for renewing commitment to Christ's church. Our deanery survey suggests that this is not yet happening in most parishes.[16]

As well as identifying non-attending roll members, the survey also demonstrated the converse: many attenders do not join the electoral roll. This is understandable in the case of Casual attenders. However, we discovered that significant numbers of frequent worshippers are also not on the roll:

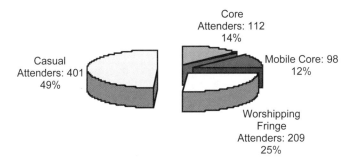

Fig 5: Categories of Attendance Amongst People who are not on the Electoral Roll in Five Survey Parishes in the Wirral North Deanery

It appears anomalous that so many who are committed to the church (because they attend regularly) have no place on the church's official, legal membership list. There is unlikely to be a single, simple explanation for the large number of core and mobile core attenders who do not appear on the electoral roll. We venture the following suggestions:

- Some are still feeling their way into Christian faith or are officially members of other churches, and are unwilling to make such a commitment yet.

- We live in an age which is shy of commitments of any kind. Many organizations (political parties for example) have seen a steep decline in numbers. Some people would rather turn up from week to week, rather than (as they see it) binding themselves to be there all the time.

- Some may never be given the chance to join the electoral roll. If electoral roll officers do not themselves attend church every Sunday, they may not be aware of new regular attenders in the church. They might offer the enrolment form only to the 'safe' people they know, while they overlook others who have been attending regularly for some time but whom the officers have not noticed yet.

In general, the information supplied by parishes indicated that attenders under 50 were poorly represented on electoral rolls. The younger age groups were *very* poorly represented. In his own parish, Paddy nags at sidespeople about the need to recognize and welcome all members of the congregation of whatever age; but the fact remains that some sidespeople wholly ignore anyone under 25 years of age and do not learn the names of congregation members under 45.

The conclusion must be that the electoral roll does not adequately identify attenders, even regular attenders.

Frequency of Attendance and 'Church Life' Membership

We gave further attention to adults over 24 years of age.[17] We asked parishes to distinguish those members who are active in church life—that is, they do more than merely attend worship services—from those who are Modal 'worship services only' members (see section on Categories and Definitions above). We cast the net wide to identify Church Life members.

We cannot be sure that all churches applied identical standards for Church Life and Modal members. We do not claim scientific precision for the distinction between involved and uninvolved Christians, yet we found that similar patterns emerged from many parishes—although there were also signs that parish policies had a noticeable effect on involvement. In most parishes, Modal members were in the majority, in the proportion 60:40. One parish, Poulton Lancelyn, was an exception—it reversed the proportions with a 60:40 majority of Church Life members.

We then cross-referred the Modal/Church Life information against attendance data. It emerged—surprise, surprise—that Church Life members were likely to be more frequent attenders while Modal members were likely to be less frequent attenders. We found that those who attend worship less than twice a month are less likely to be involved in specific roles at worship services (for example as Sidespeople, Scripture readers, intercessors, or welcomers) or take part in other aspects of church life (for example Mothers' Union, housegroups).

A two-tier community fellowship exists within the church

Our survey is a snapshot of attendance and membership patterns at a particular point in time. It cannot of itself identify trends. But this evident distinction between frequent-attending Church Life members, and infrequent-attending Modal members, leads to the following speculation: a two-tier community fellowship exists within the church. The Core and Mobile Core are likely to be 'insiders.' But the Worshipping Fringe and Casual[18] attenders may experience significantly lower pastoral engagement with their fellow churchgoers.

In turn this may leave them outside the informal fellowship groups that naturally arise and function amongst more regular attenders, and often dominate amongst the weekly congregation. They may be vulnerable to a process of further disengagement from the church. Another cause of anxiety is the fact (as mentioned above) that the Worshipping fringe and Casual attenders accounted for 49% of all churchgoers who were present during the survey (in some parishes more than 50%) but only 21% of the average weekly congregation. The more vulnerable section of the congregation may also be the less visible.

Which came first, the chicken or the egg? Our survey cannot answer the question of whether infrequent church attendance is the cause or the consequence of low involvement in a church's wider life; but it does strongly suggest that the two are connected. Worshippers who reduce their frequency of church attendance are joining a group of people which is statistically less likely to be active in the wider life of the church.

We have not given you all the numbers here. However, we found that many young adults between 24 and 40 are infrequent attenders (see Figs 3 and 4 above), and that that age band also includes a higher proportion of Modal members than other age bands.[19] This prompts a reflection. It may be that the activities of the church shape themselves for a visible, Core and Mobile Core, Church Life membership which is predominantly 40+ while only a narrow range of options is open to the 25–40 year olds apart from worship. We could complacently say that this problem will solve itself in time. The 30-year-old will get to 50, the children will leave home and then he/she will get more involved. Or we could say, *now* is the time when they need maximum support and encouragement as Christians, so how will they get it?

Midweek Worshippers
Regular and occasional mid-week services were held in several parishes.[20] Our attendance data included attenders at these services. Sunday remains the main day of worship in all the survey parishes: the numbers of mid-week attenders were relatively small—but they were significant. Almost 12% of attenders were present at a mid-week service.

People who came to a mid-week service fell into three categories:

- those who only attended a mid-week service
- those who were attending their second or third service in a week
- those who normally attended a Sunday service but attended on a weekday when they did not attend a service the previous weekend

All three categories featured in each parish, although the proportions varied considerably.

In all the survey parishes, these midweek services were 'traditional.' Typically they were services of Holy Communion—a midweek oasis of quiet spirituality. In general, these services were not perceived as thriving, dynamic growth points in the life of the church. Yet they involved contact with significant numbers of people. For some individuals, this was the *only* point of contact. Paddy confesses to having seen his parish's midweek service as a necessary chore rather than a spiritual opportunity. It can be a little gem of worship and teaching, but we rarely advertise it. Yet without trying, his parish of Barnston is in contact with 36 people at its midweek service. It is already an opportunity for mission and pastoral contact.

None of the survey parishes at present offers 'Sunday worship midweek'— that is, a major parish service into which significant resources of music, teaching and welcoming are poured, and intended for those who cannot (or will not) attend on a Sunday. We hear suggestions that there is a demand for suitable worship on a midweek evening, but our parishes have not yet plucked up courage to tackle the practical issues involved.

C. The Missionary Church

The Church and the Local Community
In every parish the overall survey attendance by members of the worshipping community reflected a higher proportion of the parish population than the weekly attendance. In certain parishes the difference was substantial. In Great Meols, for example, the parish population is 4,487. Great Meols' average weekly attendance is 102, about 2% of the population. However, their overall survey attendance was 223, which comprises a more respectable 5%.

The church is in contact with enough people to make a significant impact on the area—not just to speak to individuals, but to contribute to the life of the area.

Baptism Guests
When we consider the impact which the church makes on the local population, we need to include baptism guests as well as the worshipping community. Many churches make every effort to welcome their baptism guests both for hospitality's sake and because it is an opportunity to share the gospel. Paddy used to regard every guest as a one-off, one-time visitor. However, in an area such as the Wirral, a baptism guest is likely to reappear in church for another relative's funeral in two months' time and at a wedding next year. There is more research waiting to be done to suggest whether

occasional offices should be seen as continuing ministries rather than stand-alone events.

Barnston parish, for example, has 2% of the parish population inside the church each week, but during the survey as a whole 4% of the population came into the worshipping community. Adding in Baptism guests would give us another 1% of the parish population to make 5%. In Heswall when we add together worshipping community and Baptism guests, we find that during the survey over 13% of the parish population worshipped in an Anglican church.

3. Casual Attenders

To repeat the earlier health warning: in our jargon, a 'Casual' attender is a non-Baptism-guest, non-out-of-area-visitor who attended once during the survey. Consequently

- there is no way of knowing an individual's spiritual state from the raw attendance data

- there is no way of knowing whether this single recorded attendance is a true one-off, or whether it is part of a settled low-frequency attendance pattern such as once in three months.

Churchgoers have sometimes been perceived as being in one of two attending categories: those who go to church regularly and are part of the worshipping community; and those who turn up occasionally, normally at major festivals (for example Christmas and Easter) or other special services. Our parish surveys and studies elsewhere have shown that this is too rigid a distinction and that there is a third category in between consisting of large numbers of people who attend normal services on a less frequent basis.

Despite the health warnings above, it seems reasonable to suppose that among these Casual attenders are many with no or low present commitment to Christ and his church.[21] We may guess that this category is a mixture of people who attend with different agendas—those who are searching (both investigating the Christian faith and/or specifically examining this church) and others who are troubled by events in their lives.

The extraordinarily large numbers of Casual attenders may go almost unnoticed

We may suspect that it also includes people who were previously frequent attenders but are now drifting out of, or already feel estranged from, the main fellowship of the local church. Many of the electoral roll members who only attended once during the surveys may fall within this group.[22] The survey does not answer our questions about the Casual attenders' motivations. But whatever their personal trajectory, the survey shows that the Casual attenders are *there*, and they represent a mission opportunity.

Casual attenders by definition came only once in eight weeks. As a result in the weekly congregation they are overshadowed by more frequent attenders. However, the pie-chart at Fig 2 above showed us that in Heswall a massive 34% of all the people who worshipped in church during the survey were Casual attenders—not counting the Baptism guests. Heswall parish had the largest Casual count, but the other survey parishes also had significant proportions of Casual attenders in their worshipping community; none had fewer than 16%. However, the extraordinarily large numbers of Casual attenders may go almost unnoticed if they are distributed between several different church services.

Barnston parish provides an example of how Casual worshippers may 'hide.' During the survey, Barnston had the equivalent of three double-decker busloads of Casual attenders—not Baptism guests, but people who live in the parish and came to church just once during the survey. Surely such a large group of unfamiliar[23] people should be glaringly obvious? Not so. Barnston has six regular services per week. During the survey, the largest number of Casual attenders at any one service was 18; in many cases it was just one or two. Yet over the whole survey, their number added up to 160.

The Casual attenders include people of every age (obviously, the smallest ones being brought to church by their parents or other carers). Given the rather small numbers (in most survey parishes) of frequent worshippers in the teens-to-thirties age groups, Casual attenders sometimes represented a very significant proportion of that age group who attended.

Potentially, the Casual attenders are people through whom the local church is engaged with the local population—people with a foot in each camp. Their social circle and social activities are less likely to be dominated by churchgoing friends and church events. Through this group, the church can reach out to the local population where belief in God may be widespread but formal Christian observance is not. There are good reasons for a mission-minded church to cherish its Casual members.

However, the information from BSA and other surveys (see next chapter) points to a large loss of Casual attenders. This has serious consequences for the church's mission. A loss of Casual attenders may lead to a progressive disengagement of the church from the local population.

Reflections

3

The results of our survey, which are comparable with the results of earlier surveys mentioned above, tell us that the church is in touch with many more people than you would guess from looking at the weekly congregation.

But it is not our intention to present the numbers as some kind of success to be celebrated.

This information is not evidence of church growth, merely recognition of the real size of the local church. Church attendance is unmistakably in decline, but there are two independent variables that each contributes to falling weekly attendances: (1) reduced numbers of individuals attending and (2) changed patterns of attendance. This is not a new situation but one that has probably existed throughout the modern history of the church. However, during the last fifty years changing patterns of attendance have had an increasing impact on weekly presence, an impact that has been largely overlooked because of our focus on attendance during a single day rather than the actual worship practice of individuals. In fact there is evidence to suggest that when the Church of England started to collect regular weekly statistics in 1968 this was probably already an inappropriate indicator of the size of the worshipping community.[24]

In day-to-day parish life, we are heavily (and inevitably, and rightly) influenced by the views of those who are most evidently committed to the church's public life, the Core and the Mobile Core. But as a church in mission, we want to look wider. How can parishes respond to those who are less frequent worship attenders, the Worshipping Fringe and Casual attenders? These people, who attend less than four weeks in eight, accounted for around half of those identified during our surveys. For the majority, attendance at worship was their only contact with the church.

We have repeatedly stressed that this survey is a snapshot. It gives us some idea of where individuals were when the survey was taken, but it cannot show us in which direction they were moving. However, we have to take seriously other research which describes as common a process of leaving the church in which an individual's church attendance tails off gradually, rather than ceasing suddenly.[25] Most churches are conscious of new and unfamiliar people but perhaps we are less aware of those whose attendance has reduced and who may be heading for the back door.

The Casual Attender: A Church Leaver?

The BSA studies show that since 1983 there has been a loss of almost 2 million attenders from the Church of England. This does not mean that 2 million people, who had been going to church every week, suddenly vanished. A closer examination of the BSA data shows that the loss of those

- who attended weekly was 270,000
- who attended at least monthly was 400,000
- who attended at least once a year was 1,800,000

The reduction amongst the weekly or monthly attenders does not necessarily signify that these individuals have left the church. We offer for testing the following hypothesis: many of those who attended weekly will have reduced their frequency and moved into the monthly category, and those who attended monthly will have moved into the yearly category. We suggest that the overwhelming way the church is haemorrhaging is through the eventual exit of those who have reduced their attendance to less than once a month.

How would we ever notice the loss of Casual attenders, unless we were specially looking for them? The complicated pattern of attendances allows people to slip out of the church unobtrusively. In Barnston parish, for example, the average number of weekly attenders was 289. However, they are spread over five services on a Sunday plus a midweek service. A reduction of 1% in the overall weekly attendance would mean the loss of three people per week—which is unlikely to be noticeable spread over six services, in view of the week-to-week fluctuations in numbers. But if this loss represented three fewer Casual attenders each week, a 1% annual reduction could imply that in the course of a year we lost contact with 150 different people.[26]

Casual attenders could well include many who are still thought of as part of the church community

Casual attenders could well include many who are still thought of as part of the church community—some are even members of the electoral roll—but whose frequency of attendance has dramatically reduced. (Longitudinal study would be necessary to confirm this suspicion of reducing attendance among the people in our survey.) Significantly, many Casual attenders are under 40 years of age. Does this mean that the majority of those who are moving into and out of the church tend to be amongst the younger element in our congregations? If so, this clearly must be both a concern and challenge for each parish.

Of course, the Casual attenders also include some (many?) who are moving in the opposite direction, into church. Some have been stirred up by the Spirit of God, and are making their first contact with an institution they have hitherto shunned. Our snapshot survey cannot tell us the proportions of Casual attenders moving in and moving out (or stationary in some low-frequency attendance pattern). But we do not need to wait for more information before saying that parishes would do well to identify and pay special attention to their Worshipping Fringe and Casual attenders. Somehow we have to discern the direction of movement of each member of a potentially very large group of individuals, and develop an appropriate pastoral/missionary strategy to draw them closer to Christ.

Churchgoing, Belief and Commitment

In this context, it is relevant to mention research which has been done into the link between church attendance and the level of Christian faith and commitment. It seems to be comparatively unusual for a person to abandon faith and therefore to stop attending church. Jamieson found only one such person in interviews with 108 church leavers.[27] Robin Gill indicates that reduction in churchgoing may lead to a diminution in belief rather than the other way around.[28] Gill also suggests that amongst those who leave the church, the levels of Christian belief and values are likely to remain high for several years.

In fact it is clear from research carried out over the last 25 years that the level of religious belief amongst the population as a whole remains surprisingly high, and that whilst only a small minority actually attend church the majority still believe that there is a God, that Jesus lived, that there is an after life, and other similar fundamentals of Christian faith.[29] Grace Davie summarizes and encapsulates the situation with the phrase 'Believing without Belonging.'[30]

However, the nature of that general-population belief can be different from the nature of belief held by the majority of regular churchgoers. Whilst most non-churchgoers may believe there is a God, only a small minority believe that he is a personal God and even fewer believe that he is active in people's lives.

In any individual case there may be special reasons why a person attends church infrequently. In Paddy's parish, some active Christians are Casual attenders because they often travel overseas on business. But the research mentioned in this section suggests that infrequent church attendance is bad for a person's spiritual health. This is not in itself a surprising statement. However, if we were to find that people in our congregations are gradually reducing their frequency of church attendance, then we should be concerned. Statements such as 'They are looking for a worship pattern which suits them,' or 'Their work makes it hard for them to attend every week' or 'Other children's activities are often held on a Sunday' may be true, and may reflect accurately the pressures which afflict people in our society, but they do not break the statistical link between absence and weak belief.

There is another reason to cherish our Casual attenders. Not only are they are a point of contact with the wider community, but they may also include some Christians—perhaps many Christians—who are in trouble, whether they know it or not. Our snapshot survey does not demonstrate that this is the case; demonstration will have to await a second or subsequent survey. But when we put together the results of research on church leavers, the large numbers of Casual attenders, and the fact that many Casual attenders are electoral roll members, we have to hear a call to action.

Conclusion: Some Practical Suggestions

Our survey has helped us to look realistically at who comes to church. It has made visible a section of our congregation—the Casual attenders—which appears to be both spiritually at risk and missiologically strategic.

We have loaded our discussion with the assumption that many Casual attenders are on their way out of the congregation. It was suggested to us that Casual attenders are just as likely to be on their way in.

This suggestion is a prime candidate for further research. We have anecdotes of people who were occasional church attenders who were then invited on an *Alpha* course (or whatever), became Christians, and started to attend church more frequently. However, we do not know what proportion of Casual attenders are moving in which direction.

Yet as soon as we recognize the existence of this large body of Casual attenders, we can start to make changes which address their needs. Some have been mentioned above—reappraising preaching and teaching programmes, and revising our view of the age-profile and the level of Christian understanding in our congregations.

Some parishes in our deanery have introduced pastoral programmes (not all as a direct result of this survey). For example, one parish[31] has divided its congregation into two categories for pastoral care. The first category is people who are pastored through the regular home group/ Bible study/ small group system. Anyone not covered by this system enters a second pastoral category. In the second category, a lay pastor is responsible for up to four 'pastoral units' (individuals or families). This officer visits or telephones his/her group members regularly, and ensures that they are kept in the network of the church. The lay pastors are themselves placed in groups for fellowship and support.

Another parish has a 'link scheme,' with four or five observers in each congregation, who hold a list of known congregation members. Once a month the observers meet for breakfast and compare notes about who has come new to church, and which existing members are missing. Some parishes consciously exploit the coffee rota and the flower rota, by inviting fringe members to take part: someone with a task in the church is more likely to identify with the church, as a prelude to believing.

Paul Simmonds, from Coventry Diocese, offers further practical suggestions:

- Obtain the names and addresses of all church members including Casual attenders. (This was a valuable spin-off from the survey cards). Have an attractive welcome card in the pews.

- Learn from the children's leaders, who keep lists of names and addresses of those who attend and those who are missing, and can visit and provide spiritual support to those on their books. (This is the root of the success of the Kidz Klub model.)

- Obtain email addresses (the survey cards again!) and use them to keep Casual attenders in touch and make them feel cared for. A well-designed message template helps. Note that people ought to be made aware that they may be contacted when they give information on welcome or survey cards.

- Attach every identifiable Casual attender to a house group or cell group for prayer and to maintain contact.

- Have a baptism team. Make the follow-up of baptism families and their guests part of the team's responsibility.

- Invite Casual attenders to *Alpha* or *Emmaus* courses.

- Run regular newcomers' events (maybe a tea, possibly hosted in a Casual attender's home).

Every church or parish will be able to plan an appropriate strategy to make effective contact with its own Casual attenders. But nobody will make any plan until they are persuaded that the Casual attenders are there—and that is the purpose of this booklet.

Note: Setting up a Survey

We encourage parishes, deaneries and other levels of church organization to consider running their own surveys. Many of the basic principles for arranging a survey can be gathered from the text above. They include:

- Discussion with and support from PCCs or other relevant bodies. This survey can only be successful (produce meaningful data) with the wholehearted co-operation of a large number of people. A lot of time may be required to explain the purpose of a survey, allay any fears and fine-tune its administration.

- Selecting a suitable length for the survey. We worked with an eight-week period. A longer period would have produced even more interesting information—but conscientious collection of data, and its subsequent processing, would have become burdensome.

- Selecting a suitable period in which to hold the survey. We tried to avoid major festivals because of the distortions in attendance pattern which these are thought to create.

- Having adequate trained personnel at every level to run the survey, including handing out and collecting survey cards and entering and analysing data.

- Being aware of and respecting data protection protocols.

- Constant, repeated, clear communication with congregations on every occasion when the survey is being administered. There will be some newcomers present even in the last week of an eight-week survey. Service leaders can wreck the whole exercise by getting bored with explaining it at every single service: 'you all know by now what these survey cards in the pews are for.' No they do not!

John now has considerable experience in setting up and analysing attendance surveys—not only the one reported in this booklet, but others which he has been asked to help with. He will be glad to offer advice to enquirers who email him at sur-miss@freeuk.com.

Notes

1 See *The Times*, 5 February 2002

2 P Brierley, *The Tide is Running Out* (Christian Research, 2000) p 129

3 See R Currie, A Gilbert and L Horsley, *Churches and Churchgoers* (Clarendon, 1977) p 128; *Church Statistics*, booklets published by the Central Board of Finance of the Church of England for 1996 and 1998, and *Church Times* for 8th February 2002.

4 Data from the BSA Surveys 1983 to 1999 is available from the Data Archive at Essex University.

5 R Warren, *Signs of Life: How goes the Decade of Evangelism* (Church House Publishing, 1996) pp 46–47.

6 Notable resources are surveys in a deanery of the Diocese of Wakefield (1997), in most of the Diocese of Ripon and Leeds (1998) and in eighteen parishes of the Diocese of Canterbury (1998). Some information about these surveys is published in R Warren and R Jackson *There Are Answers* (Springboard, 2001) in S Cottrell and T Sledge, *Vital Statistics* (Springboard/Archbishops' Council, 2002) and in R Jackson *Hope for the Church* (Springboard 2002). The National Centre for Social Research provides annual data (available from the Data Archive at Essex University) independent of churches and religious organizations which comprise a longitude series that show changes since 1983. The findings of all these surveys are consistent with one another and with the results of our own survey in Wirral North (2000–2001) which is summarized in the present booklet.

7 Compare the BSA survey for 1999, which reported that a million people attended worship at an Anglican church every week, but that more than 2 million attended (excluding weddings, funerals and baptisms) during a month. The other church-based surveys mentioned came up with similar ratios.

8 A word of caution: in any individual case, the apparent pattern seen over eight weeks may not be representative of the person's medium-term habit of church attendance; see section 'Built-in limitations.' But we have to start somewhere.

9 For information on conducting a parish survey, see the Note opposite on page 26.

10 The question of data protection was addressed from the beginning. For information on data protection issues, please contact John Roberts at sur-miss@freeuk.com.

11 Those who would like to discuss the statistical backing for statements in the text are invited to contact John Roberts by email at sur-miss@freeuk.com.

12 In most cases. One parish, Bebington, supplied data without identifying individuals to John. This restricted the analysis he was able to give to this parish's data.

13 The age groups used for children in our surveys are not identical with local population data, but they are nevertheless sufficiently close to draw comparisons.

14 P Brierley, *Religious Trends 2000/2001 No 2* (Christian Research 1999) p 2.15.

15 Membership of the electoral roll is voluntary but is open to anyone who has reached the age of 16 years and who is a baptized and declaring member of the Church of England. Those who live outside the parish must also be habitual worshippers.

16 New Ferry was the exception, with its high proportion of electoral roll members attending worship.

17 The previous age-band (17–24) includes people of student age whose attendance and involvement is likely to be disrupted by long spells away from home.

18 See definitions at the start of this chapter.

19 The picture was somewhat variable from parish to parish.

20 Patterns of midweek worship were much more variable between the parishes, and from week to week within each parish, than Sunday patterns.

21 This is certainly a possible implication of the Modal *vs* Church Life information discussed on page 16 above.

22 Five of the parishes had significant proportions (15% to 37%) of electoral roll members among Casual attenders. New Ferry was the only parish where this was not the case. There is evidence to suggest that most departing worshippers do not stop churchgoing immediately. See note 26 below.

23 But see Chapter 3. Casual worshippers are not all unfamiliar faces.

24 In *The Myth of the Empty Church* (SPCK, 1993) p 323, R Gill gives the diocesan average weekly attendance for Ripon and Leeds as a percentage of the population at 3.3% in 1968, 2.7% in 1978 and 2.3% in 1989. The *'People Count'* report on the diocesan wide attendance surveys at Ripon & Leeds gives the weekly average attendance (14,000 people) as 1.9% in 1998, a figure consistent with the decline experienced over the previous thirty years. However, the overall survey attendance during a month in 1998 (34,000 people) represented 4.9% of the population. This monthly figure of 4.9% in 1998 is almost 50% greater than the weekly figure of 3.3% thirty years earlier in 1968.

25 'The vast majority of those who were interviewed did not leave their church suddenly. In fact they indicated a gradual process of reflection, questioning and withdrawal which lasted many months or years prior to their decision to leave. They drifted out of the church, often realizing only in hindsight that they had left. Because of the nature of church participation it is possible to drift out on a trial basis, or change your attendance patterns to the point of being increasingly less regular at church events.' A Jamieson, *A Churchless Faith* (SPCK, 2002) p 32.

26 …assuming that each Casual is a one-off attender. That may well not be the case, but you see the point we are making.

27 A Jamieson, *A Churchless Faith,* p 42.

28 R Gill, *Churchgoing and Christian Ethics* (Cambridge University Press, 1999) pp 38, 65–66.

29 There is widespread evidence of this from different research projects. R Gill gives details from various surveys in *Churchgoing and Christian Ethics*. Information from the British Social Attitude Surveys is given by Roger Jowell *et al*, in *British Social Attitudes: The 17th Report*, 2000 (Sage Publications) p 124.

30 G Davie, *Religion in Britain since 1945* (Blackwell, 1994) pp 4–5.

31 Upton, not one of the survey parishes.